To Jeremy, who grew up in St. Andrews, and his children Theo, Lydia and Bartholomew.

With best wishes,

from Rosemarie

30th. November, 2000

To Jonathan, Kate and Daniel
who grew up in St Andrews.

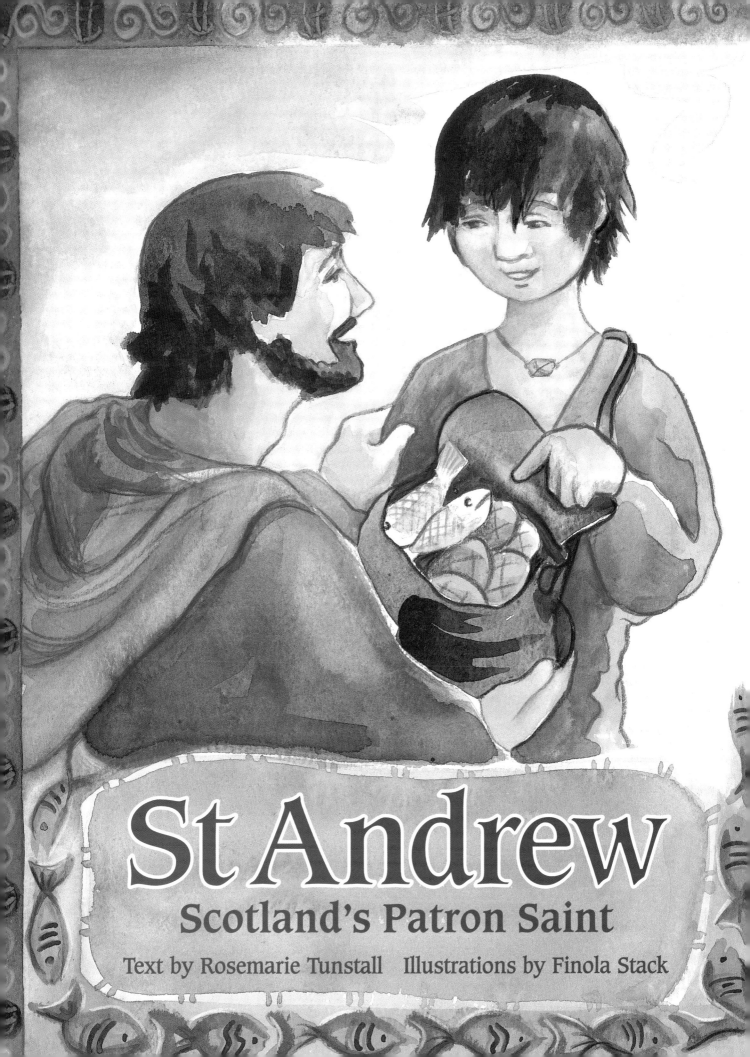

St Andrew

Scotland's Patron Saint

Text by Rosemarie Tunstall   Illustrations by Finola Stack

St Andrew's life was shaped and inspired by the teachings of Jesus Christ. It is therefore essential to tell Andrew's story in close relation to this. Leckie & Leckie have endeavoured to ensure all references to the Gospels of the New Testament are accurate.

P. 3
'Come, follow me, and I will make you fishers of men.'
is taken from **Matthew 4:19**.

P. 8
'...but how far will they go among so many?'
is taken from **John 6:9**.

Many thanks to Reverend Ted Collington, and Reverend David Lewis for their advice. The publisher is especially grateful to Reverend J.L. Leckie for a lifetime of immeasurable support and inspiration.

St Andrew
Scotland's Patron Saint

Text copyright © Rosemarie Tunstall 2000

Illustrations copyright © Finola Stack 2000

Published by Leckie & Leckie Ltd, 8 Whitehill Terrace, St Andrews, Fife KY16 8RN, Scotland
Tel: 01334 475656 Fax: 01334 477392
E-mail: hq@leckieandleckie.co.uk
Web: www.leckieandleckie.co.uk
Leckie & Leckie is an Investor in People Company.
®Leckie & Leckie is a registered trademark.

Project management and editing by David Nicoll

MADE IN SCOTLAND
Printed by Inglis Allen, Kirkcaldy, Fife on 100% recycled paper.
Page layout by Redgate Creative, Cupar
Scanning by Elements, Edinburgh

ISBN 1-898890-13-7. A CIP catalogue record for this book is available from the British Library.

This Book Belongs To

In the first century, a fisherman called Andrew lived by the Sea of Galilee.

This sea is in the north of the country that we now call Israel.

Capernaum

Mt. Carmel

Nazareth

GALILEE

Sea of Galilee

Nain

River Jordan

Joppa

Jericho

Jerusalem

Bethlehem

Hebron

the Dead Sea

Masada

Beersheba

Andrew spent his days fishing with his brother Simon Peter. They had been born into a Jewish family. The Jewish people were waiting for a special person promised by God to come and be their leader.

One day Andrew and Simon Peter were casting their nets into the sea when a man called Jesus approached them.

'Come, follow me, and I will make you fishers of men,' he said.

Andrew and his brother believed Jesus was the leader they had been waiting for. Jesus taught them, along with ten other men, about the love of God.

They helped the poor and sick and became known as the twelve disciples of Jesus.

Andrew shared everything he learned from Jesus with many people. They believed, like millions of others today, that Jesus Christ is the Son of God.

People who believe in Jesus Christ and follow his teachings are called Christians.

Jesus had the power to do amazing things known as miracles.

Andrew was with Jesus when one of the most famous miracles took place by the Sea of Galilee.

Five thousand people had gathered there to listen to Jesus. There were no villages close by to get food from, so later they became hungry.

Andrew looked around for food but could only find a boy who had five small barley loaves and two small fishes.
'...but how far will they go among so many..?' Andrew wondered.

Jesus thanked God for the food, divided it and gave it out. There was enough for everyone with a further twelve baskets left over too!

Some people thought
Jesus was dangerous and
opposed him. They did not
believe he was the
Son of God.

He was put to death on
an upright cross.

Christians believe Jesus came back to life after three days and returned to be with God in heaven.

They also believe God then sent his Holy Spirit to help Andrew and the other disciples.

The men travelled to many countries to talk about their faith in Jesus.

However, not everyone agreed with what they heard.

'That's a lie,' they would say and sometimes the disciples were cruelly treated.

This happened to Andrew and he too was put to death on a cross, like Jesus, but people think Andrew's cross was a diagonal shape.

He was buried in Patras in Greece and later his bones were moved to Constantinople in Turkey.

After his death, Andrew was made a saint in honour of his special Christian life and works.

In the fourth century it is said that an angel appeared to a monk called Rule. The angel told Rule to take some of Andrew's bones from Constantinople and sail west. They were said to be the bones of three fingers, one upper arm, one kneecap and a tooth!

For hundreds of years the bones or belongings of well-known saints were thought to be very important. They were called relics.

'They will bring us
good fortune, protect
us and cure our
illnesses,' people said
and they kept them.

During Rule's voyage, his ship sailed into
violent storms. It was thrown about by
huge waves and forced to land near a
town on the east coast of Scotland called
Kilrymont. This later became known as
St Andrews in memory of the disciple.

Rule managed to save the relics and bury them in St Andrews. In the twelfth century a church was built near-by called St Rule's in honour of the monk, who had also been made a saint after his death.

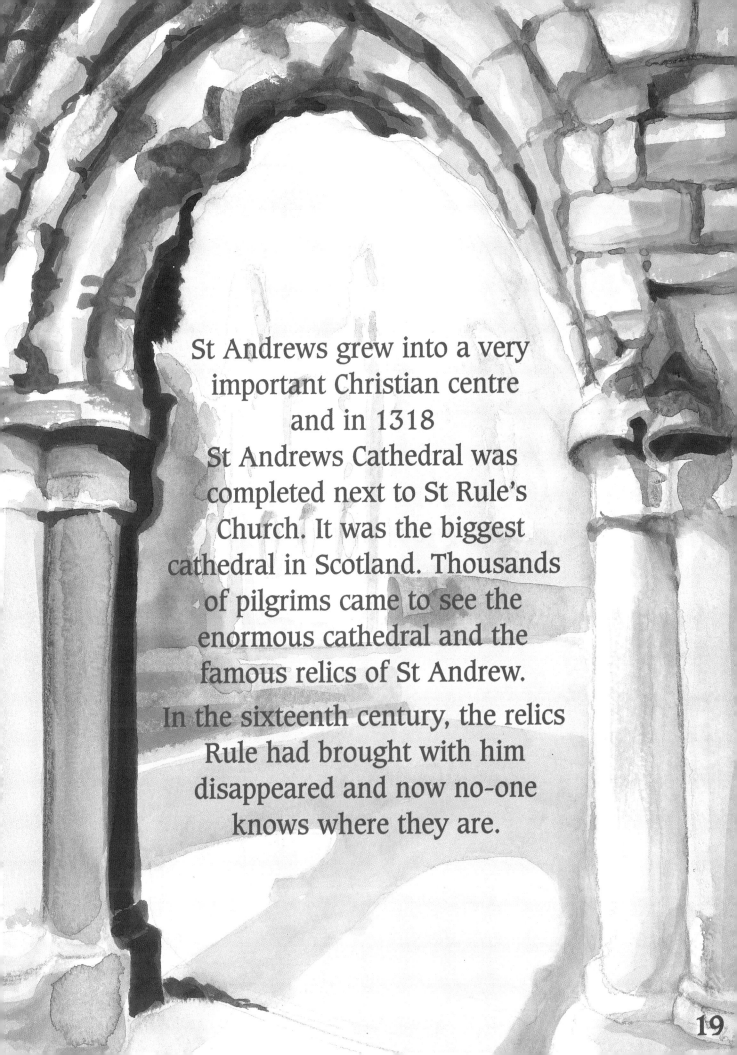

St Andrews grew into a very important Christian centre and in 1318 St Andrews Cathedral was completed next to St Rule's Church. It was the biggest cathedral in Scotland. Thousands of pilgrims came to see the enormous cathedral and the famous relics of St Andrew.

In the sixteenth century, the relics Rule had brought with him disappeared and now no-one knows where they are.

Today many visitors enjoy walking around the beautiful ruins of St Andrews Cathedral.

The tower of St Rule's Church also stands today and you can climb all 157 steps to the top to see wonderful views of the town of St Andrews, the sea and the surrounding countryside.

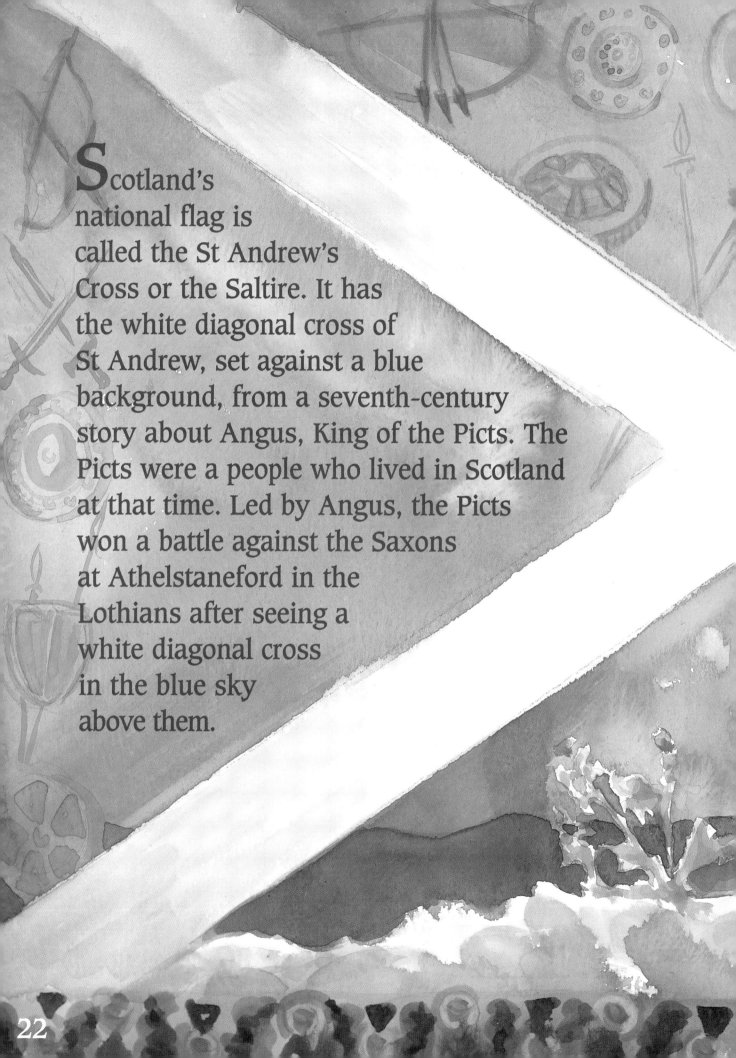

Scotland's national flag is called the St Andrew's Cross or the Saltire. It has the white diagonal cross of St Andrew, set against a blue background, from a seventh-century story about Angus, King of the Picts. The Picts were a people who lived in Scotland at that time. Led by Angus, the Picts won a battle against the Saxons at Athelstaneford in the Lothians after seeing a white diagonal cross in the blue sky above them.

Over the centuries, St Andrew and the Saltire became widely used by Scots as symbols of their country.

Today we see the colours of the Saltire in many places - on Scottish car stickers, sports strips and even on the faces of some rugby and football supporters! They like to paint it on before international matches.

24

Throughout the world Scottish people celebrate St Andrew's Day on the 30th November. On that day, Saltires fly on many buildings and special events take place reminding everyone of St Andrew, Scotland's Patron Saint.